WITHDRAWN

LIMA PUBLIC LIBRARY
650 West Market Street
Lima, Ohio 45801

W9-ATJ-471

CARNEGIE
LIBRARY
D. P.

Writing SECRET CODES and Sending HIDDEN MESSAGES

Writing SECRET CODES and Sending HIDDEN MESSAGES

by GYLES BRANDRETH

ILLUSTRATED by PETER STEVENSON

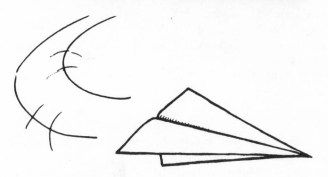

Sterling Publishing Co. Inc. New York

Edited and designed by Vilma Liacouras Chantiles

Library of Congress Cataloging in Publication Data

Brandreth, Gyles Daubeney, 1948–
  Writing secret codes and sending hidden messages.

  "Original edition published in Great Britain by
Carousel Books . . . under the title 1000 secrets: the
greatest book of spycraft ever known"—T.p. verso.
  Includes index.
  Summary: Explains how to use secret codes, including
Morse, Caesar's, Sandwich, Resicrucian, and others, as
well as how to send hidden messages using invisible ink,
how to take fingerprints, and other tricks and techniques
  1. Ciphers—Juvenile literature.   2. Cryptography—
Juvenile literature.   [1. Ciphers.   2. Cryptography]
I. Stevenson, Peter, 1953–   ill.   II. Title.
Z103.3.B7   1984   011.54'36   83-24230
ISBN 0-8069-4690-3
ISBN 0-8069-4691-1 (lib. bdg.)

American edition published in 1984 by Sterling Publishing Co., Inc.
Two Park Avenue, New York, N.Y. 10016
Original edition published in Great Britain by Carousel Books, text
copyright © 1982 by Gyles Brandreth, illustrations copyright © 1982 by
Transworld Publishers, under the title, "1000 Secrets: The Greatest
Book of Spycraft Ever Known."
Distributed in Canada by Oak Tree Press Ltd.
c/o Canadian Manda Group, P.O. Box 920 Station U
Toronto, Ontario, Canada M8Z 5P9
Manufactured in the United States of America
All rights reserved

j652
B

Contents

LIMA PUBLIC LIBRARY.
MAIN LIBRARY

8608262 L

INTRODUCTION

Did you know that Julius Caesar had a secret cipher still used to this day? That a lemon can be one of the most valuable pieces of equipment for writing a hidden message? Or that Morse code can be sent in writing, by knotting a rope, or flashing a lamp?

In this book you can learn how to write secret messages by Morse code, Caesar's cipher and many other useful systems. Use the codes at home, when shopping, visiting your uncles and aunts, on a trip, at the beach or on a boat—anywhere, anytime.

Have fun with your friends and family by learning new code techniques. You'll stretch your brain power by memorizing ciphers and using them daily. After you pick out codes you like, this book helps you write them with invisible inks—ordinary lemon or apple juice, milk or starch you have at home. Then your friends can develop the messages by tricks given in the book. You can learn how to take fingerprints and develop them and how to keep a special book for all your codes.

Writing Secret Codes and Sending Hidden Messages is divided into 15 easy-to-read chapters. There are jokes and signs, facts and hideouts, language and equipment tips and more. You can find these tips by using the "secret key" symbols next to each tip. If you want to read about codes, for example, just look for the symbol. Memorize the symbols on the opposite page and you will find your information quickly. Then you will be on the way to learning all about secret codes and messages, using your brain and having fun at the same time.

SECRET KEY:

 CODES & CIPHERS

SECRET MESSAGES

 DISGUISES

INVISIBLE INKS

 TECHNICAL DATA

STORIES OF REAL SPIES

 LANGUAGE

SIGNS

 HIDEOUTS

JOKES

 FACTS

EQUIPMENT

PLEASE DO NOT MEND BOOK
Return to Library for Repair

Healthy, Stealthy and Wise

You must know the area where you live like the back of your hand. So obtain a map of your local area and study the roads and landmarks very carefully.

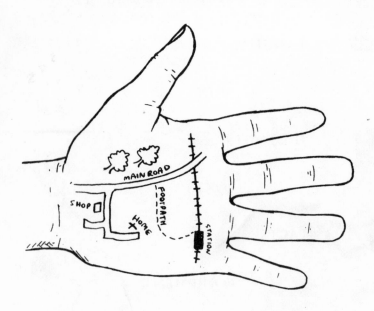

It is a known fact that a coder or decoder needs more brains than muscle. It is good to be strong, but it is not always quite as simple as fighting your way out of a situation. Instead, you need to think. Just a little bit of thought can go a very long way.

Test your memory by looking at a photograph, or a person in the street for two seconds. Then try and build up an "identikit" picture of him using different noses, chins, eyes and other features drawn on small pieces of paper; then arrange them to find the best likeness.

Sport is a very good way of keeping fit. So after writing codes, relax and play a team game.

When are you like a bird of prey?

When you watch someone like a hawk.

When you wake up each morning, stretch each muscle in turn, raising your arms and legs up towards the ceiling. This will wake you up and make you feel fully alert.

A coder must develop a very good memory. If he has not and writes everything down it is possible that the written material could fall into an enemy's hands, even if written in code. But what is in your head only, nobody can steal.

 Breakable pieces of equipment can be kept inside old socks for protection.

Many exercises can test your memory. One simple method is to study a tray with twenty objects on it. Study the tray for two minutes only. Then, without looking at the tray, say or write down everything that you remember seeing.

If you have a pile of papers on your desk, draw a thin pencil line down the edge of the pile. If the line is crooked on your return you will know that someone has been through your papers.

Test your friends' knowledge of codes by writing out a well-known poem in code and see who is the first to tell you the poem.

What do you call an ape with a gun?

Sir.

Keep a list of all the car numbers of the vehicles that are regularly parked in your area. You will then be able to spot a strange and unknown car when it appears.

Try this test at your headquarters. Send one friend out of the room. The rest pick someone to be an "enemy agent." The one sent outside must then come in and try to discover who the agent is. He can ask what questions he likes but the others can only answer "yes" or "no." Only the "enemy" agent is allowed to lie. Having been found out, the one chosen as the enemy leaves the room next and the operation is repeated.

Draw a map of your area on a large piece of cardboard, and using the pieces from a Monopoly game, put in all the houses and buildings.

11

This card game is a great mental test to improve your memory. Spread a pack of cards out face downward on the floor. Take turns at picking up two cards. **You must pick up two cards that are the same**—two aces, two twos, two kings, two queens, and so on. If you do pick up a pair, then you keep them. If you do not pick up a pair, you must lay them down again. This is where your memory will be tested, for you could lay down a king of hearts, and two turns later pick up a king of clubs—if you can only remember where you laid the king of hearts you will have a pair! The one with the most cards when the whole pack has been picked up will be the winner with the best memory.

Coder: Doctor, doctor, I keep thinking I'm a dumpling.
Doctor: *Don't get into such a stew.*

Measure your own height from head to toe every three months. If you know exactly how tall you are, you can estimate how tall your friends are.

Why are rich bankers successful?

Because they have a lot of cents (sense).

To disguise your voice, try changing the accent. Speak in broken English, or pretend that you are foreign and cannot speak English at all.

 If you carry an umbrella with you, it can be lowered to cover your face whenever necessary so that nobody will be able to spot who is behind it.

Give yourself a rosier complexion by rubbing rouge into your cheeks.

To improve your skill at code
breaking, try filling in a crossword
puzzle using a particular code.

Good powers of observation are essential.
When you have some free time with nothing
to do, take a notebook and go and sit in some
public place and watch people.

In twenty years of records, Thursday has proved
to be the wettest day of the week. So do not
make any plans for a Thursday which will be
spoiled if it rains.

Test your powers of observation by looking at a
magazine picture of a man for two seconds.
Close the magazine and try to write down exactly what he was wearing, the color of his eyes,
hair, whether he had a beard, moustache,
glasses, etc.; also what he carried, what he wore
on his feet, and any distinguishing marks. Then
look back at the picture and see how good your
observation was.

Coders have to be clear-thinking and smooth-talking. Test yourself with this top-secret tongue twister: "Caesar sees the 'C' in Caesar's cipher." Say it five times without making a single mistake!

What happened when the Frenchman jumped off a bridge?

He went in Seine (insane).

If you are spying on someone in a park on a sunny day, sit on a bench and pretend that you are asleep. If your quarry comes too close for you to keep on pretending, then hide behind a newspaper. Two very small slits cut into your paper will help you to see through it and continue watching.

Morse, of Course, and a Few Secret

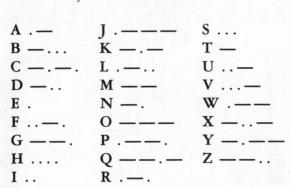

Morse code is one of the most famous codes of all time. It is made up of dots and dashes. Each letter of the alphabet is replaced by a specific number of dots and dashes and can either be written, or tapped out (two quick taps for a dot and four for a dash). Or it can be flashed with a torch in the dark (one flash for a dot and a longer beam for a dash). Here is the internationally used Morse code:

A	.—	J	.———	S	...
B	—...	K	—.—	T	—
C	—.—.	L	.—..	U	..—
D	—..	M	——	V	...—
E	.	N	—.	W	.——
F	..—.	O	———	X	—..—
G	——.	P	.——.	Y	—.——
H	....	Q	——.—	Z	——..
I	..	R	.—.		

? ..——..

Period .—.—.—

Here is a secret message in Morse code.
What does it say?

— —. — — — .—. —.. — — — —.

.. ...

—.—. . — — — — — .. —. — — —.

It reads: GORDON IS COMING

A tree is a great hideout if it is large enough for you to hide behind. Look around for any holes which you can see through. Wear camouflage on your hat so that you can move your head without being spotted.

A secret message in Morse code can be tapped out on the ground to a nearby contact with a stick. Or if the ground happens to be sandy or muddy then the message can be tapped out on a stone or tree trunk.

A whistle can be used to send messages in Morse code.

Any instruction not written in code is known as a **CLEAR MESSAGE.**

A **code** is usually made up of letters, words, signs, numbers or symbols. This means that a single word can represent a whole sentence.

Anyone who searches out information is called a **mole.**

Morse code can also be written as a series of peaks, **low peaks for dots, high peaks for dashes:**

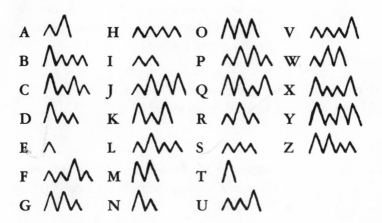

 Decipher this secret message:

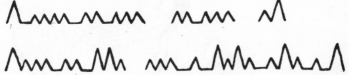

It reads: THIS IS A BIG SECRET.

Send Morse code messages from a room with the light on by flicking the curtain up and down. A small flick for a dot and a longer one for a dash. If your contact is carefully positioned outside he or she will get the message.

How did the Vikings send secret messages?

By Norse code.

A secret message in Morse code can be tapped out on a radiator or water pipes to someone in the next room.

An old doorbell can be screwed down to a piece of board and used to send messages in Morse code.

A message in Morse code can be flashed from a window by covering the bulb on a table lamp with your hat.

Why did the chicken cross the road?

For some foul reason.

Code Mode

A group of coders who work together are known as a **code ring**.

 Give each member of your ring a code name. It is best to choose a theme, so that perhaps the master will be FOX, his contact will be RABBIT, an agent will be HARE, a courier BADGER, and so on.

Issue each member of your ring an identity card with his photo, fingerprint, and code name. Each member must show you his identity card at the start of each meeting.

Fool the enemy by keeping your secret codes written in a **code book**. This should be a copy of any book, a book of fairy stories for example, in which you have pasted blank pages on which you write your codes. The book can then be hidden in your bookshelves.

A secret code book can be made from absolutely any book. As long as you and your contact each have a copy of the same book you will be able to send secret messages. Simply find the words of your message in the book and give the page number, the number of the line (starting from the top of the page), and the number of words from the left along the line. All you have to do is find the page and count, for example, seven lines down and the third word along on page 23 for the first word of the message.

A message will look like this:

**32.10.2   71.14.9   63.7.1   77.13.8
62.12.3   10.2.1**

Remember, the sequence should be: **Page — Line — Word**. Unless your contact knows that, he might get the wrong message!

To completely fool everyone, place a book on your bookshelves clearly marked *Secret Code Book* and fill it with meaningless letters and symbols.

Snapping your fingers together is called a **"FILLIP."**

Choose a special symbol for your own code ring. This symbol can appear on your note-paper, your own secret documents, your identity cards and so on. The simplest method is to use a stamp of some kind. (See page 120 for an idea.)

 Make sure that you have a **cipher clerk**—someone who is responsible for deciphering all your messages and who can write down all your codes and ciphers in a special secret code book. This is a very responsible job.

If you are pinning maps, instructions or messages on the wall in your hideout, pin them on the same wall as the window. Then anyone looking in through the window will not see them.

 The radio was invented by Marconi, who also invented a special secret code to go with it.

To devise your own code, write down the alphabet and then get each member of your code ring to think of different symbols for each letter. When each member of your ring then learns the code, you will have a unique method of communication that even an experienced cipher clerk will have difficulty in breaking.

Can you decipher this?
TNEGA YMENE NA YB DELIART GNIEB ERA UOY

It reads: YOU ARE BEING TRAILED BY AN ENEMY AGENT.

Test your agents' abilities at decoding messages by having a race to see who can break a code first.

Anyone who teaches a friend his skills and the art of code craft is known as a **trainer**. Anyone who is learning how to be a coder is called a **trainee**.

Anyone who carries messages or orders is called a **courier**.

When you write a message in code you **EN-CODE** it. When you work out what a code means you **DECODE** it.

When cracking a code, write it in very large letters with large spaces between the lines. Then as you begin to crack the code you can write the message underneath the code words.

 Big X: I'm looking for a spy with one eye called James Bond.
Big Q: *What's the other eye called?*

A useful way of sending codes is to use a dictionary. Or any book will do as long as you and your contact have the **same** book. Go through the book and look for the first word of your message. For example, the word could be "**Have**"— this might be the **8th word** on **page 52,** so write down the page number followed by the word on the page. Now look for the next word of your message and write down the page number of that, until you have completed your message. A dictionary is a good book to use because it contains all the words you will need. A copy of *Alice in Wonderland* might pose problems if you want the word "counterintelligence"!

A message using this code will look like this:

32.58 71.108 63.44 77.98 62.91 10.12

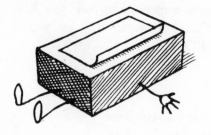

A prearranged place for delivering or picking up a message is known as a **dead letter box.**

Secret messages can be hidden inside leaves! It sounds difficult, but it's not. Take a large leaf and roll it around a pencil and secure it with an elastic band. Leave the leaf in a box or drawer to dry. When it has dried out you can carefully remove the elastic band and the pencil and the leaf will stay as a hollow tube. Inside you can hide rolled up messages and leave them at a drop. Even if the drop is searched, nobody will take any notice of a dried-up leaf.

In leaf code, a small twig pushed through the center of a leaf could mean **"meet me tonight as arranged."**

If you develop a leaf code of your own, bend over a leaf and push the stalk through the top of it—so that a tube is made. This could mean **"danger ahead."**

Invent a secret knock as a code. Your members can tap on the door when they are outside. If you hear this secret knock, you will know that it is a member of your ring outside and you can safely let them in. If you hear a strange knock you will know that it is not a member outside and the door should only be opened with very great care.

Coders should be fashion conscious and should be able to look very smart when mixing in elegant circles. If the occasion calls for a top hat, then this can be used to hide cameras and small pieces of equipment underneath.

To fool everyone, jumble up letters at random to make it look like a real code. This is known as a SPOOF CODE. Your family and friends will spend hours trying to decipher it.

A special **code grill** can be made very easily. All you do is take a piece of cardboard and cut out some holes. Write an ordinary looking letter which incorporates the words of your message, with the words strategically placed so that when the grill is placed over the top just the words of the message appear.

If a secret agent was captured and abandoned in the desert why wouldn't he starve to death?

Because of all the sand which is there.

Modern technology may be clever, but no one has yet invented a computer which can crack codes. Of course, computers can help, but it still needs a person's brain to help because the art of cracking codes really is a case of having a lot of patience and using trial and error.

Try to find a good strong metal box such as an old cookie tin. Put inside it code books and any documents that must never be found. Hide the box where it is unlikely to be found.

When on a mission in the country, you can disguise yourself as a scarecrow. Wear some old clothes, a battered hat with some straw hair. Practice standing very still.

A wooden rod or cane will be a useful piece of equipment if disguised as a scarecrow. Simply push it through the sleeves of your jacket, across your back, and it will support your arms. A broom handle is ideal.

Two crossed twigs, or a broken twig is a sign meaning, "Do not go any farther."

If you think someone may have cracked one of your codes, write a message and leave it at your usual drop. (If it disappears you will know that a stranger knows where your drop is.) In this spoof message say that you have a new drop, in a hollow tree, for example. In a hollow tree place a fake message of jumbled-up meaningless letters. If this message disappears, too, you will know that the stranger read your first message and has cracked your code. Now that you know that, you can drop that code and use another one. Also find a new secret drop in which to leave your messages.

Any assumed or false name that a coder adopts is known as an **ALIAS**.

The very best coders always write to each other in a different code as this gives them practice in deciphering so that they can easily recognize a code when they see one.

A secret message can be sent by placing the syllables **IP** after each consonant in your word. So, the word DOG becomes **DIPOGIP,** and CAT becomes **CIPATIP,** and so on.

To find out which direction the wind is blowing, take a look at a dog. Before lying down a dog will turn around in circles to learn which way the wind is blowing and face the wind to scent danger.

If you have a dog he can help you in your mission by hiding secret messages for you. If you can train him well enough he might bury secret equipment. Or if he is clever, his sense of smell might enable him to track down a stranger for you.

Blankety Blank
and Other Messages

Milk can be used as an invisible ink if you use it undiluted. To read the message, warm the paper gently with an electric iron set on "**low**," and the writing will appear brown.

If you ever use chemicals to make invisible inks (and you may have a chemistry set that contains the right chemicals for this), always treat each substance as if it were HIGHLY DANGEROUS. Never ever taste any of them and always wash your hands when you have finished using them.

Sodium chloride (table salt) can be used as an invisible ink. Add one heaping teaspoon to a glass of warm water. Stir until the salt dissolves; when cool, it is ready for use.

A very effective invisible ink can be made from **lemon juice.** Simply squeeze out some of the juice and use it instead of ink. When it dries, the paper will appear blank. To read the message, simply warm the paper gently with an electric iron, and the writing will appear brown.

 Half a teaspoonful of ordinary **laundry starch** in a quarter cup of water can be used as an invisible ink.

Rather than writing a whole message in invisible ink, an ordinary and innocent-looking letter can be written with particular words underlined or circled in invisible ink to spell out the message. When your friend receives the letter, he has only to heat the paper and the ringed words will appear and give him the message.

 An invisible ink substitute can be a piece of **candle** or white wax crayon. Use it to write your message. To read the message, rub over the paper with a wax crayon of a different color and the writing will appear.

What do you call a cat that chews lemon drops?

A sour puss.

 When you write letters that have a message in invisible ink hidden between the lines, be sure to end your fake letter with your own special code to let your contact know what it has been written with. If you end the letter **"Yours sincerely"** it means **lemon juice** has been used; **"Yours truly"** means **milk** was used; **"Yours faithfully"** that a **sugar and water solution** was used; and **"Very sincerely yours"** could mean that **salt water** was used.

Strawberry jam diluted with a little water makes an excellent ink.

 Squeeze **grapefruit juice** out from the fruit and use as an ink. Develop the message by heating the paper. If you have a grapefruit for breakfast, you can write the message then, pretending that you are writing a shopping list or merely jotting down things that have to be done that day. That way no one will suspect anything.

A few teaspoonfuls of **sugar** in a glass of warm water makes a quick and easy invisible ink. The writing will appear brown when the paper is warmed.

Ordinary **tap water** can be used as an ink in an emergency. Write your message with it and allow the paper to dry completely. To develop the message brush over the paper with diluted ink (one teaspoonful of ink to a small glassful of water) the writing will appear in a darker color of the ink than the rest of the paper.

Always mix invisible inks, especially chemical inks, in a disposable container. NEVER mix them in a drinking glass or you are likely to get poisoned.

Believe it or not, **onion juice** is a very good invisible ink. The juice can either be squeezed out, or you can push a toothpick into an onion and write with the toothpick. The smell is sure to put the stranger off the scent!

Any **fizzy drink,** such as orange soda or lemonade, will make a good invisible ink. Write your message and allow it to dry—it will be invisible. To read the message, warm the paper gently and the writing will appear brown.

A very good ink can be made from **epsom salts.** Just mix a little of the powder with some water. The only disadvantage of this ink is that it does require quite a strong heat for the message to appear, so it is not an ink to be recommended unless it is the only substance you have.

A secret message can be written on a piece of paper using a **wax candle.** To read the message, sprinkle powder or sand onto the paper—it will stick only to the wax and so allow you to read the message.

Goat's milk and evaporated milk make just as good an invisible ink as cow's milk.

Most pharmacies sell a **styptic pencil,** which is a stick of alum people often have to stop bleeding if they cut themselves shaving. You can use it to write a secret message. Warm the paper and the message will appear.

A chemical called **bicarbonate of soda** (baking soda) is used quite frequently in the home, for cooking. You may have some in your own home. If so, mix it with just a little water and it can be used as an invisible ink.

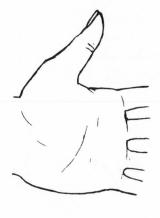

When writing with invisible ink always keep your fingers at the point where you finished writing when you need to dip into the ink. This will help you find your place again.

Apple juice can make a fairly effective invisible ink, but not as good as citrus fruits. There could be times when all that you have with you is an apple so make use of it. You can eat the apple afterwards!

When writing with invisible ink, don't send your message as a blank piece of paper, as this looks highly suspicious. Instead write an ordinary looking letter in ordinary ink, and write your message using invisible ink **between the lines.**

When writing with invisible ink it is usually best to write with a strong toothpick. Sharpen the end slightly by rubbing it against a brick wall or a piece of sandpaper.

If you unscrew a ballpoint pen, you will find there is room inside to conceal a piece of paper if you roll it up. Secret messages can then be carried in what looks just like an innocent pen.

When sending a message in invisible ink (and remember you should never send a blank piece of paper), have a symbol on the paper so that your contact knows how to develop the message. An "H" for "heat," "P" for "powder," and so on.

Add one teaspoonful of **honey** to a glass of warm water. Allow the mixture to cool and use as an invisible ink.

A piece of tape along the envelope's edge on any letter you send will make it extra secure and will prevent anyone from steaming the letter open.

If no invisible inks are available you can use the **watermark method.** Soak a sheet of paper in water and lay it flat on a sheet of glass or a mirror. Place a sheet of dry paper on the top and write your message in pencil or with a ball-point pen. After writing your message, destroy the top copy and allow the bottom piece of paper to dry. When it is dry it will look like a perfectly ordinary piece of plain paper. **But** if you wet it again the message will appear on the paper like a watermark, and will disappear when the paper dries.

If an invisible ink calls for a chemical developer, place the paper directly into the developer downwards. Do not move it about or the message will smudge. To read the message, lift it straight up.

Windmills in France and Belgium were used to send secret messages during the First World War. For example, this position of the blades might be an SOS.

Making an invisible message appear is known
as **DEVELOPING**.

> **To read a message written in invisible ink,
> hold the paper against a radiator or just
> above an electric lamp. NEVER use a
> match, and always take the greatest care not
> to burn yourself.**

> If you don't have a radiator, lay the invisible
> message on top of a **warm,** not hot, toaster-
> oven or oven when your parents are using
> them. Cover the invisible message with a dry
> pot holder or towel and rest it for ten minutes
> or until the message turns yellow. (**Don't** put
> the message **inside** the oven.)

Powdered graphite is an excellent powder developer for messages written in wax and can be
bought at most hardware stores. Its real use is
for lubricating locks.

> To develop secret messages written in wax,
> place some powdered lead from a pencil sharp-
> ener in a little cloth bag and rub the bag gently
> over the paper. The message will then appear.

If a secret message is wet with the developer,
lay it on a sheet of blotting paper. In this way
you will not damage the furniture.

> If you find in a book a recipe for an invisible
> ink you may see the word "**DEV**" (meaning
> "develop"). This will tell you how to read the
> message—whether you have to heat the paper,
> brush it with a solution, etc.

Occasionally it may be necessary for you to copy a document. But you may not have a camera with you. Do not despair. There is a very secret formula that will allow you to copy documents without a camera. This is how you make it:

One teaspoonful of liquid detergent
One teaspoonful of turpentine
Two teaspoonfuls of water.

Using a sponge, brush or tissue, wipe this solution over the document you wish to copy. Press a piece of plain white paper onto the document and press *really hard.* Carefully lift off the piece of white paper and you will find a copy, in reverse, of the document. To read it all you have to do is hold it in front of a mirror. **The secret is to press very hard.** Rubbing the document with a spoon helps. Practice at first with a newspaper article until you become really experienced.

If you look in a book of invisible inks and see the letters **F** or **P** beside a bottle, these letters stand for "Fugitive" and "Permanent."

 Fugitive means that you will have to warm the paper to read the message and when the paper has cooled it will disappear again.

Permanent means that once you have developed the message, the writing will remain visible, such as if you put powder on a message in wax.

 Take care never to spill invisible inks onto your clothing or onto the carpet.

Sly A-B-Cs

A **cipher** is a system where every letter in the alphabet is substituted by another letter, number or symbol. When people refer to secret codes they usually mean a cipher.

Alphabet ciphers are the most popular of all ciphers. Here is one that is used quite frequently. All the letters that use straight lines appear first, followed by those that have curved lines:

Alphabet: A B C D E F G H I J K L M N O P Q R
S T U V W X Y Z
Cipher: A E F H I K L M N T V W X Y Z B C
D G J O P Q R S U

Take the message: **JO IS HIDING**
It will read: **TZ NG MNHNYL**

Decipher this secret message:
LZ JZ BADNG NXXIHNAJIWS

It reads: GO TO PARIS IMMEDIATELY

43

The **Vowel cipher** will confuse your pals! The five vowels, as you know, are **A E I O U.** When you write a message change the vowel to the next in the sequence, so that **A** becomes **E,** **E** becomes **I,** and so on.

The message: **USE YOUR EQUIPMENT AS ADVISED** will look like this: **ASI YUAR IQAOPMINT ES EDVOSID.**

Simple to decipher **when** you know the secret!

Decipher this secret message:
UAR CUAROIR HES BIIN EBENDUNID

It reads: OUR COURIER HAS BEEN ABANDONED.

When is a getaway car not a car?

When it turns into a driveway.

The sounds which carry best and are easiest for the human ear to hear are, "**ah,**" "**eh,**" "**ee,**" "**aw**" and "**oo.**"

To make your *own* code write each letter of the alphabet on a different piece of cardboard. Jumble the 26 cards and lay them out in a row. The first card becomes "**A,**" the second "**B,**" and so on. Write down the code so that you remember it.

There are many English words which are used more frequently than others. It is useful to know which occur most frequently because one or two of these words will appear in almost every secret message. Here are the top thirty words, which should help you when deciphering messages:

FROM	AT	HAD	HER	I	IN
HAVE	AS	WAS	HIS	HE	OF
THAT	IS	AND	YOU	BY	ON
WITH	BE	ARE	BUT	OR	A
THE	IT	NOT	FOR	TO	WHICH

In written English, the letter **E** occurs most frequently.

When deciphering messages remember that **Z** is the least common letter of the English language.

What sort of spy appears frequently at Christmas?

A mince spy.

"Jackdaws love my big sphinx of quartz" contains all the letters of the alphabet. It can be used to test your knowledge of secret codes, because to write it in code you will need to know every symbol, letter or number.

How could the decoder tell the weather with a piece of string?

If it moved about it was windy, if it was wet it was raining.

In the English language there are certain letters that frequently occur together, such as **QU** and **TH**. This should be remembered when decoding messages.

An umbrella is always a useful piece of equipment. It can be used in self-defense if ever necessary!

Why did the messenger put sugar under his pillow?

He wanted sweet dreams.

Coders often talk in a language of their own—
DOUBLE TALK or **DOUBLE SPEAK.** Use
ordinary innocent sentences which have a totally different meaning to your members.

In **DOUBLE TALK** the sentence "It is
sunny today" means "There are a lot of
strangers around."

In **DOUBLE TALK** the sentence "It will
rain later today" means "There will be a
meeting this evening."

Knock, knock.

Who's there?
Ivor.
Ivor who?
Ivor you let me in the door or I'll climb
through the window.

Here are the top twenty groups of two letters
that frequently occur together:

TH	IN	ES	OR	HE
AN	RE	ER	ON	AT
ND	ST	EN	OF	TE
ED	TI	HI	AS	TO

Here is one of many alphabet ciphers:

Alphabet: A B C D E F G H I J K L M N O P Q R
S T U V W X Y Z
Cipher: B D F H J L N P R T V X Z A C E G I
K M O Q S U W Y

Take the message:
**COLLECT SECRET PARCEL FROM THE
AIRPORT**
And it becomes:
**FCXXJFM KJFIJM EBIFJX LICZ MPJ
BRIECIM**

What does this secret message say?
TCPAK FCHJ ABZJ RK FBJKBI

It reads: JOHN'S CODE NAME IS CAESAR

A Transposition cipher is a cipher in which all the letters of the message are left the same but the order is jumbled up. A few null letters are sometimes added to make it harder to break.

What did the bald barber say when he was given a comb?

I'll never part with it.

A unique cipher is called the **Double Dutch cipher.** You can use the basic principle of it to develop your own cipher. All you have to do is choose a syllable, such as **IP,** and add it after every consonant in your word.

Create your own **Double Dutch cipher** by creating your own syllables, such as **OP, OD, AT, IK,** etc. and placing them after consonants in your message.

Develop your own code with colored handkerchiefs. A red handkerchief in your top pocket could mean **danger,** green could mean **all is well,** etc.

What is black, has six legs, wears a disguise, and listens to people?

A secret bug.

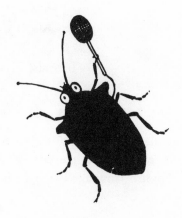

A **consonant**—such as **b** or **p**—is a letter of the alphabet which cannot be sounded by itself. A consonant is combined with a vowel to make a syllable.

A clever secret code is called **OPISH,** in which the letters **OP** are placed after every consonant. The word BOY becomes **BOPOYOP** and GIRL becomes **GOPIROPLOP.**

A variation of the **Double Dutch cipher** is to take whatever syllable you choose (say **IP,** for example) and place it in front of every vowel of your message. The word **ESPIONAGE** would becomes **IPESPIPIIPONIPAGIPE!** The word **DISGUISE** becomes **DIPISGIPUIPI-SIPE.** You can use any syllable you wish.

Can you decipher this secret message using the above cipher?
CLINAINUDINE INIS INOINUT INOF ININK INAGINAININ

It reads: CLAUDE IS OUT OF INK AGAIN

When deciphering messages, remember that more than 50 percent of all words in the English language begin with the letters **T, O, A, S,** and **W.**

A code that has been in use in England for over three hundred years is known as **Trevanion's code.** It is quite simple to use and very effective. All you have to do is send a quite innocent-looking letter. To read your message your contact will take out every third word following a punctuation mark. This simple message:

Dear Sid,

We will leave our dog at your house this week, and come after him again later in the week. Probably at midnight owing to the late arrival of our train.

See you tomorrow,
Tony

Gives you the secret message: **LEAVE AFTER MIDNIGHT TOMORROW**

How do you dress on a cold day?

Very quickly.

Caesar's Cipher
and Other Greats

Julius Caesar invented a cipher known as **Caesar's cipher.** Although our alphabet has more letters than his, we can still use his method. In this cipher each letter of the alphabet is replaced by the letter that comes **three** places before it:

Alphabet: A B C D E F G H I J K L M N O P Q R
S T U V W X Y Z
Cipher: X Y Z A B C D E F G H I J K L M N
O P Q R S T U V W

By using this as a guide you can write your own secret messages.

Decipher this using the above method:
YFD U FP XOOFSFKD QLJLOOLT

It reads: BIG X IS ARRIVING TOMORROW.

A **Substitution cipher** is a cipher in which a plain letter, symbol, figure or number is substituted for each letter of the alphabet.

Decipher this secret message:
NFFU TBOEZ JO UIF QBSL BU GPVS P DMPDL

It reads: MEET SANDY IN THE PARK AT FOUR O'CLOCK—each letter is replaced by the one that follows it in the alphabet.

Alexander the Great was one of the first people to use ciphers extensively for secret communication. It was in the days when paper scrolls were used. But the message was not on the paper. Instead, it was on the wooden baton in the center of the scroll.

 Philip II of Spain, in the time of the Spanish Armada, is said to have used a cipher that contained 500 different symbols.

Where would a coder deliver a message in his sleep?

In a spring.

You can hide behind a hat with a wide brim.

To disguise your voice, try talking with your tongue either in front or behind your bottom teeth. You will find it gives you a completely new voice.

How do you make a Maltese cross?

Stand on his toe.

Loosening your collar means **"Mission accomplished."**

One of the most famous ciphers is called the **Rail Fence cipher.** Take your message:
THE CODE WORD IS WASHINGTON

Now write it on two lines like this:

T E O E O D S A H N T N

H C D W R I W S I G O

Finally divide the letters into groups of four. If your message does not divide equally by four then add a few extra letters on the end. These meaningless letters are known as "**nulls.**" So, your message will read:

TEOE ODSA HNTN
HCDW RIWS IGOR

Can you decipher this message? It is in Rail Fence cipher.
AEEY GNIT ALNM NNMA ETSR IIGE

It reads: AN ENEMY AGENT IS TRAILING ME

It is very difficult to disguise your laugh, so listen carefully to people's laughs so that you can recognize them.

A simple **Roman cipher** was used in the time of Julius Caesar by using the number code system, substituting letters of the alphabet with Roman numerals:

A	B	C	D	E	F	G	H	I	J	K
I	II	III	IV	V	VI	VII	VIII	IX	X	XI

L	M	N	O	P	Q	R	S
XII	XIII	XIV	XV	XVI	XVII	XVIII	XIX

T	U	V	W	X	Y	Z
XX	XXI	XXII	XXIII	XXIV	XXV	XXVI

Can you decipher this message?

XVI IX III XI XXI XVI
XIII V XIX XIX I VII V
VI XVIII XV XIII XIX V III XVIII V XX
IV XVIII XV XVI

It reads: PICK UP MESSAGE FROM SECRET DROP

A great breakthrough in modern technology was the invention of the **microdot**. A whole typewritten page can be reduced to the size of a full stop.

Enthusiasm is an important quality to have even when you feel really exhausted.

An alternative **Roman cipher** is to write the Roman numerals in reverse order, instead of starting at I:

A	B	C	D	E	F
XXVI	XXV	XXIV	XXIII	XXII	XXI
G	H	I	J	K	
XX	XIX	XVIII	XVII	XVI	
L	M	N	O	P	
XV	XIV	XIII	XII	XI	
Q	R	S	T	U	
X	IX	VIII	VII	VI	
V	W	X	Y	Z	
V	IV	III	II	I	

The message: **ESCAPE QUICKLY** would read:
XXII VIII XXIV XXVI XI XXII
X VI XVIII XXIV XVI XV II

Decipher this secret message:
II XII VI   XXIV XXVI XIII
XIII XII IV   XXIV IX XII VIII VIII
VII XIX XXII
XXV XII IX XXIII XXII IX

It reads: YOU CAN NOW CROSS THE BORDER

You can tell if a watch is very old because the Roman numerals for the number 4 are expressed as IIII and not IV as on more recent clocks and watches.

If you are in disguise, be sure to avoid any dogs that you may know. They will recognize you immediately and rush over to greet you and give you away.

Knots to You!

Secret messages can be left lying around in the form of knots on a piece of string. An ordinary loop knot can make the equivalent of a *dot* and a knot in the figure-eight manner will give you the equivalent of a *dash*. A whole message in Morse code can be put on a piece of string in this way.

Secret messages can be concealed in the knot in your tie if you fold the paper up into a small square.

Morse code messages knotted onto a piece of string have an added advantage: You can feel the knots with your hands and so "read" the message in the dark.

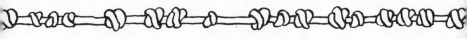

A coder who is good at knitting or embroidery can develop a **secret code** of his or her own. Different series and sequences of knots and stitches can convey an entire message. An innocent-looking scarf could contain a highly secret piece of information!

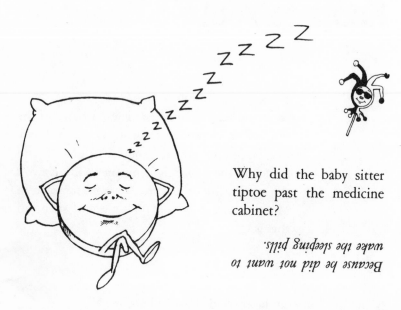

Why did the baby sitter tiptoe past the medicine cabinet?

Because he did not want to wake the sleeping pills.

If you wish to use a code that will really confuse your friends, however hard they search in books, you can always develop one of your own.

What did the shoemaker say to the chiropodist?

My fate is in your hands.

The **Sandwich code** has been used for centuries. Why it is called that? The reason is that you make a sandwich with the letters. Take your message:
MEET ME BEHIND THE OLD BARN AT MIDNIGHT

Separate the letters:
M E E T   M E   B E H I N D T H E   O L D   B A R N   A T M I D N I G H T

Then sandwich some meaningless letters in between.
MBEFEHT   MYED   BGEAHLIPNFD TYHJE   OPLWD   BGAWRKN   ADT MVIXDPNAIRGJHCT

To decipher the message you must take out every other letter.

In his book *A Tale of Two Cities,* Charles Dickens created a character called Madame Defarge who used to sit and knit beside the guillotine during the French Revolution while heads were being cut off. Her knitting, however, was a form of passing secret messages because the various stitches she used were her very own secret code.

Decipher the following secret message:
CFABNRCYEKL THOMNGIDGWHMTSS MLEREYTKIGNFG

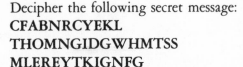

It reads: CANCEL TONIGHT'S MEETING

The Domino code is sometimes called the **"Rosicrucian code."** It works like this:

A B C	D E F	G H I
J K L	M N O	P Q R
S T U	V W X	Y Z

Use a little grid as above. Each letter of the alphabet is indicated by the type of box in the grid. A dot identifies the location of the particular letter being coded. For example:

A ⌐̣⌐   N ⊡
B ⌐•⌐   P ⊏̣
C ⌐̣⌐   X ⊓•

Take the message:
RETURN TO HEADQUARTERS NOW

It would look like this:

Decipher this secret message:

It reads: MESSAGE HAS BEEN DECODED

Change your walk by taking very big strides. Place your hands behind your back and keep your head in the air as you go. This will make you look taller than you really are.

Why did the messenger scratch himself?

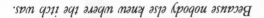

Because nobody else knew where the itch was.

If you saw the following message you would soon realize that it is a code of some kind:

GARY EDWARDS TOLD OLLIE UNDERWOOD THAT NORA ONCE WISHED

But can you see how to crack the code? It is easy when you know how—just take the first letter of each word and you can read the message: **GET OUT NOW.**

Did you hear about the man who made himself a new boomerang—and then went mad trying to throw the old one away?

A cipher, known as the **Gibb cipher,** will really fool everyone. Simply replace each letter of the alphabet with the letter that comes after it. **A** becomes **B, B** becomes **C, C** becomes **D,** and so on.

The word **CODING,** for example, becomes **DPEJOH,** and **WRITING** is **XSJUJOH.** It's quite FBTZ, isn't it! To decipher it you simply replace each letter with the one **before** it in the alphabet.

Decipher this secret message:
BO FOFNZ BHFOU JT DBSSZJOH B DBNFSB

It reads: AN ENEMY AGENT IS CARRY-ING A CAMERA

Practice walking around your house as silently as possible, learning how to cope with creaky floorboards.

A very easy code to use involves a simple change in the way you write your message. No letters are changed or substituted at all. Instead of writing your message across, write it in two columns. Take the message:

TERRY IS COMING IN DISGUISE THIS AFTERNOON

and write it:

T	G
E	U
R	I
R	S
Y	E
I	T
S	H
C	I
O	S
M	A
I	F
N	T
G	E
I	R
N	N
D	O
I	O
S	N

Take the letters row by row and place in groups of four:

TGEU RIRS YEIT SHCI OSMA IFNT GEIR NNDO IOSN

What do you call a man with very good manners?

You would say he is a-gent.

Touch and Tell

No two people have the same fingerprints. Even those of identical twins are different. So, when you have collected a person's fingerprints and you have them on record, you will always be able to use them to identify that person.

What does a good fingerprinter have between his eyes?

Something that smells.

When you leave your hideout, always wipe the door handle or knob with a cloth. On your return you can test for fingerprints to see if anyone has tried the handle.

Although no two fingerprints are identical they can be divided into four groups.

Here are the four basic types of fingerprint:

1) **Loops** — the lines all bend in a loop, like a hairpin.

2) **Whorls** — there is a complete circle in the center, surrounded by more circles.

3) **Arches** — there is an arch at the center and the lines around it curve in the same way.

4) **Composite** — a mixture of types.

 To take your agents' fingerprints, use their index finger. Roll the finger from left to right on an ink pad, pushing the finger down firmly at the same time. Immediately remove the finger and roll it again from the left side to the right side on a piece of paper and you should get a clear print. Take care not to smudge it.

To **"lift"** fingerprints, dust the object they are on gently with talcum powder. Press a piece of transparent tape on the print and clearly peel it off. If you then place the tape on a piece of black cardboard or paper you will be able to see the print very clearly.

To practice your skills at tracking, it is useful to study all kinds of tracks and footprints. Valuable equipment includes a piece of **cardboard** and some **plaster of paris** (available from model and art supply shops).

If you see an animal track in the ground, place a circle of cardboard around it (a paper clip will hold the cardboard together), and pour the plaster into the cardboard and into the track. Before it sets, put a piece of string into the plaster. This will enable you to hang it up later. After about thirty minutes, the plaster will have set. Lift it from the ground, clean away any mud, and you should have a perfect plaster cast of the footprint.

THOUGHT FOR THE DAY: It's better to keep your mouth shut and let people think you are dumb than open it and prove them right.

When you follow someone, or look for certain clues to help you discover someone's whereabouts, it is known as **tracking**.

To test your tracking skills, practice on a wet beach with a friend. Footprints will show up quite clearly in the sand. Study the soles of your friend's shoes. Close your eyes and let him "escape." After three to four minutes open your eyes and try to find out where he is by studying his tracks. Then repeat the operation, but this time *you* escape.

 Tie a bundle of twigs to a piece of string and trail them behind you when walking in the country. That way no footprints will be left.

If you ever have to cross a patch of mud, always walk backwards. This will leave a false trail and totally confuse everyone.

If you happen to be studying someone's footprints and notice that they are slightly deeper on one side, it generally indicates that he or she is carrying something heavy.

When dogs follow a man's trail they follow the scent he leaves in each of his footprints. Even humans can follow a fresh trail if it has been left on a firm floor, and if they are prepared to go down on all fours and sniff!

 If you are walking only a short distance wear a pair of adult boots. Whoever sees the tracks will look for someone much bigger than you.

The tongue prints of cows are unique, just like our fingerprints. No two cows have the same tongue print.

The plaster cast of a footprint is called a **"negative cast"** because the print appears like a bump outwards.

To make a **"positive cast"** (which will look exactly as the print did on the ground) keep the cardboard around your "negative cast" and grease this mold with petroleum jelly or soapy water, and pour in some plaster of paris and allow it to set. When it is set, you can separate the two halves of the cast. You now have a perfect print that will last forever and will help you identify any tracks you see. If you know which animal made the track—a cat, dog, cow, horse, fox, badger, or whatever—then label the cast clearly. Gradually you will be able to build up a whole collection.

When stepped on, the sand of Kauai in Hawaii makes a noise like a dog barking.

Knock, knock.
Who's there?
A messenger who couldn't reach the doorbell.

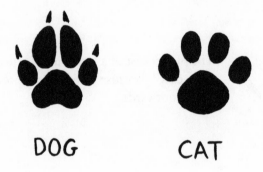

DOG   CAT

You can tell quite simply the difference between the tracks of a dog and cat: A dog print will have claw marks, a cat's will not (cats draw their claws in when they walk).

The pad of a dog's footprint is usually triangular, while a cat's is round.

Flags and Wags

When you have mastered the art of codes and ciphers, you can develop your own code in which one single word replaces a whole sentence.

Using code words, **SAUSAGES** could mean "Meet at the hideout," whereas **FRIED SAUSAGES** might mean "Meet at the main headquarters."

One code that is often used as a hand signal with flags is called **semaphore,** but it can also be used as a written code, too. The symbols are well known, as are the Morse code symbols, but you can vary them. Below are the symbols in the form of a clock face:

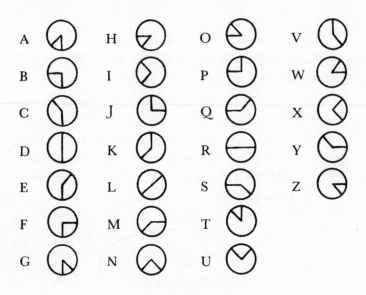

So the word **ESPIONAGE** would be written like this:

Semaphore flags can be made using two sticks and two handkerchiefs.

The position of the hands on the clock can be copied with your arms, using flags if you wish to use the Semaphore code as a proper signal. Remember to keep your arms perfectly straight all the time.

Can you decipher this secret message?

It reads: DANGER

Semaphore flags can also be made with two canes, or an old broom handle cut in half. Staple or sew onto each stick a piece of red cloth. Make two identical flags and you will then be able to send semaphore messages.

Secret messages in semaphore can be made even clearer by using two different colored flags—red and green, for example.

When a friend folds his arms, it means, "**I need protection.**"

A secret code known as the **Bi-Rev code** looks
very complicated, but is quite simple:

Take the message—
JOHN IS A DOUBLE AGENT

Divide it up into groups of two—
JO HN IS AD OU BL EA GE NT

Now write each pair backwards—
OJ NH SI DA UO LB AE EG TN

And put it back together again—
OJNH SI D AUOLBA EEGTN

Using the Bi-Rev code, try and decode the
following message:
**HTM ESAETS RYP SI OCIMGN
OTINHGT**

It reads: THE MASTER SPY IS COMING
TONIGHT

People who devise secret codes and ciphers are
called **cryptographers.**

Anyone who solves secret codes and ciphers is
known as a **cryptanalyst.**

What part of the army could a baby join?

The infantry.

A simple but effective secret code is to write
each word backwards. So, the message:
**MEET BEHIND THE LIBRARY
SHELVES**

Would read:
**TEEM DNIHEB EHT YRARBIL
SEVLEHS**

A good way of leaving a sign for a friend is to
use ordinary leaves. Choose fairly large leaves
and put them in places where they will not
arouse suspicion, but where your contact will
see them.

Why do Soviet men always work fast?

Because they are rush'n'.

The **Pig Pen code** is an unusual code. No one knows how it got its name, but it has nothing to do with pigs! With this code each letter of the alphabet is substituted by a symbol. If you are an observant coder, as you should be, you will realize that it is not a code at all but a cipher!

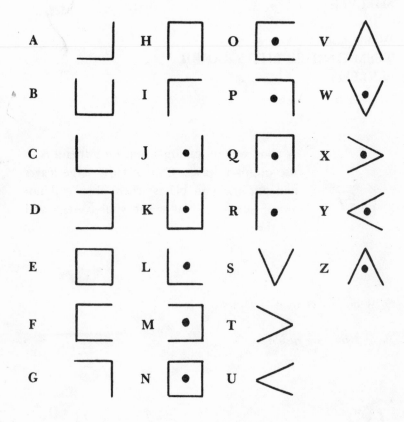

Decipher the following secret message:

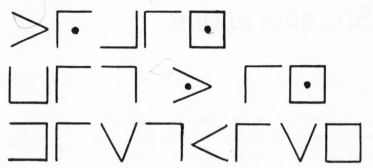

It reads: TRAIN/BIG X IN/DISGUISE

When you visit an antique shop you will often see little tags on objects. If you look at these tags you will see that they have a *code* written on them, not a price. This is because everything in the shop is a different price. Because there is no set price on an antique, the shopkeeper can really charge what he wants. The secret code tells him what he paid for the object, so obviously he must not ask for anything less. If the customer looks rich, the shopkeeper can ask for a much higher price than if the customer is obviously poor.

When do secret agents work in shops?

When they are working on **counterespionage.**

Snooperscope

A secret message can be hidden in the hollow part of an ice-cream cone. You can pass it to your contact without arousing suspicion.

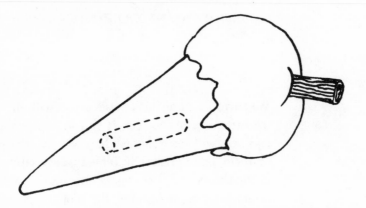

Secret messages can be concealed in newspapers or comics. Write the message on a piece of paper and tape it to a page inside the newspaper. The newspaper can be left on a park bench or sticking out of a rubbish can for your contact to pick up and read.

Decoder: You need glasses.
Friend: *How do you know?*
Decoder: I could tell as soon as you walked through the window.

 If you are upstairs in your headquarters and your contact is outside, a secret message can be sent to him concealed in a paper airplane.

Special messages can be sent to friends by hanging different colored handkerchiefs on your clothesline.

 Coder: "I can keep a secret. It's the people I tell it to who can't!"

When leaving messages in places known as "dead letter boxes," the dead letter box must be somewhere that your contact will normally visit. (There would be no point in leaving a message under a table mat in an expensive restaurant if he only eats at McDonald's, in a train if he travels by bus, at a movie if he spends his free time at the football field.) The less suspicious the dead letter box the better.

A very useful **two-way radio** can be made from two old tin cans and a length of string. Make sure that the tin has no sharp edges—it is important that a coder is in perfect health so you must not cut yourself on a tin. Put a small hole in the bottom of each can, thread the string through and tie a knot. If each person has a can and pulls the string very tight it is possible for one friend to speak into his can and be heard by the other if he puts his ear to his can.

If you see a letter **K** on the ground it is a sign to indicate the direction you should take. It acts as an arrow. **Я**

Always put long clothes onto hangers when you are not wearing them. Otherwise they will be crumpled and creased when you want to wear them and you will look highly suspicious.

Measure your arm span, from fingertip to fingertip with your arms stretched as far apart as possible. Now you know the measurement; use it when you are out on a mission and need to know a specific measurement.

 There are times when a written or verbal message could be intercepted, in which case a messenger uses a **silent signal**.

What does a coder do when an enemy's nose is running?

Put his foot out and trip it up.

During the First World War, village women used to carry secret messages hidden in a basket of eggs. They looked so innocent that soldiers allowed them across the border, and even if they searched the basket they would find only an ordinary basket and eggs that were whole with no breaks or pinpricks in the shells. So where were the messages hidden? The messages were actually inside the eggs.

This amazing secret was discovered by German agents. You can learn the secret yourself. This is what you do: Obtain from your local drugstore a powder called **alum.** Mix a little of this with some vinegar. Using this substance, write your message on the egg shell. When the writing dries, the message will disappear. All you have to do now is hard-cook the egg and the message will go through the shell and amazingly appear on the white of the egg inside. To read the message you have to break the shell. (Don't eat these "message" eggs.)

If you think an egg may be hard-cooked and contains a message (by the method described above) try spinning the egg. Only hard-cooked eggs will spin.

Use a pet dog to carry secret messages! Tuck a message under his collar and take him for a walk in the park. When you meet your contact, he can bend down to pat the dog, and while stroking him can skillfully remove the message at the same time.

If you need to take a map anywhere with you, draw it on a very thin piece of silk or polyester and you will find that it can be screwed up into a very small ball and concealed on yourself.

Why did the messenger avoid the cemetery?

He wouldn't be seen dead there.

In the First World War secret agents used pigeons to send secret messages. They strapped a message to the pigeon's foot, although this was not always very reliable. Sometimes a pigeon could take days to reach its destination, or never arrive. Some experiments were tried with miniature cameras that would take pictures as the pigeon flew over enemy territory, but again this was not very successful and the idea was abandoned.

What do cats strive for?

Purr-fection.

During the reign of Louis XV of France there was a very powerful spy called **Madame de Pompadour.** She developed a technique which is used even today. This really is **TOP SE-CRET**—modern governments put wax seals on confidential documents, just as they did in the time of Louis XV, because to open and read the document you have to break the seal. So what Madame de Pompadour did was take an impression of the seal from which she could make exact copies of the original. She then broke the seal and read the confidential information. Later she replaced the seal with an identical one, made from her cast of the original. The document would then be sent to its destination apparently untouched, because the seal was intact.

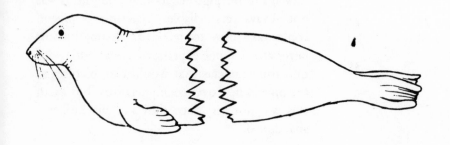

When laying a test trail use a piece of chalk and use a series of prearranged signs to show your friends the way.

What do you call a messenger in bed?

An undercover agent!

If you tape or glue a small mirror into a diary you can use it to look at what people over your shoulder are doing while pretending to look in your diary.

A secret message can be written on a large sheet of paper and that piece of paper folded into the shape of an envelope. Inside this envelope you can put a fake letter. If it is intercepted by anyone, they will read the paper inside and would never think of looking on the inside of the envelope.

Small messages can be tucked inside a picture frame.

Always carry a newspaper or comic with you when you go out. It could be useful to hide your face behind.

Secret messages written on a piece of paper can be hidden inside your shoe. If you think an enemy may search you, then a **false shoe sole** can be made by drawing around your shoe, cutting it out and placing it inside your shoe. The message can be hidden underneath where nobody would ever think of looking.

Which is the most shocking city in the world?

Electri-city.

An American spy called **Rose Greenhow** in the nineteenth century used to carry cleverly concealed messages. Even if she was searched, the messages were not discovered. Some were embroidered as a pattern on her clothes, others were in the soles of her shoes. Sometimes messages, sewn into tiny silk squares, were rolled into the curls of her hair. A lot can be learned from Rose Greenhow's secret methods.

When coders meet and are given facts, information or instructions, it is called a **BRIEFING.**

Secret messages and documents can be carried in a record cover belonging to an LP. The message can be inside the cover and you can easily pass the cover to your contact saying: **"Thanks for lending me your record. I enjoyed listening to it."**

In the year 500 BC a secret agent called Trimalcio set out on a mission, leaving behind him a trail of seeds so that he could find his way back. Or if he got into danger, his contacts could follow the trail which would lead them to him. Unfortunately, Trimalcio was captured by the enemy and the seeds were eaten by wild birds. Trimalcio was never seen again.

Never leave an edible trail or spy sign. If you do, some wild animal is sure to eat it. Twigs or pebbles make good signs.

When out on a mission it is always a good idea to take some food rations with you—something easy to carry such as peanuts or dried fruit.

Send secret messages by writing your message on the top right-hand corner of an envelope and stick a large stamp over it. If a stranger intercepts the mail he will look at the letter inside and find nothing. Your contact can steam the stamp off the envelope to read the message underneath.

Knock, knock.
Who's there?
Snow.
Snow who?
Snow use, I've forgotten.

Number Letters

 Number ciphers are easy and fun to use. Simply take each letter of the alphabet and number it. Here are two ciphers you can use:

Cipher 1

A	B	C	D	E	F	G	H	I	J	K	L
1	2	3	4	5	6	7	8	9	10	11	12

M	N	O	P	Q	R	S	T	U	V	W	X
13	14	15	16	17	18	19	20	21	22	23	24

Y	Z
25	26

Cipher 2

A	B	C	D	E	F	G	H	I	J	K	L
26	25	24	23	22	21	20	19	18	17	16	15

M	N	O	P	Q	R	S	T
14	13	12	11	10	9	8	7

U	V	W	X	Y	Z
6	5	4	3	2	1

To write the message, use numbers in place of the letters.

Here is a secret message using one of the two number ciphers. What is the message and which of the two ciphers is being used?

7 19 18 8 14 22 8 8 26 20 22 18 8 4 9 18 7
7 22 13 18 13 24 18 11 19 22 9 7 4 12

It reads: THIS MESSAGE IS WRITTEN IN CIPHER TWO

I have five noses, six ears, and four eyes. What am I?

Very ugly!

The symbol for a dollar is a modified version of the symbol stamped on the old Spanish "pieces of eight."

There are many number ciphers, as we have already seen, but you do not have to use the numbers 1–26 just because there are 26 letters in the alphabet. You can use absolutely any numbers you wish, like this:

A	B	C	D	E	F	G	H	I	J	K
297	298	299	300	301	302	303	304	305	306	307

L	M	N	O	P	Q	R	S	T	U	V
308	309	310	311	312	313	314	315	316	317	318

W	X	Y	Z
319	320	321	322

The message: **LOOK OUT** would read:
308 311 311 307 311 317 316

Unless the decoder actually knows the cipher, it is incredibly difficult to work out.

A coder poses as a salesman in a candy shop. He is four feet, eight inches tall, and wears size six shoes.
What does he weigh?

Candies.

With many secret codes and ciphers the words are split into groups of *four* letters so that each word looks the same and does not give any clue to its meaning. If the message will not divide equally into four, then extra letters or numbers are added to make up the number and confuse anyone trying to break your code.

In the Arctic an ordinary conversation can be heard seven miles away. So beware!

When trying to decode a message, try to discover which letters are the vowels. All words have vowels. If you see a word of one letter it usually means it is a vowel. Once you have established which are the vowels, you will find it quite easy to crack the code. For example:

X LXKQ XCQ CRQZM

Now the first word is of one letter. Assume that **X = I** which would make the message look like this:

I LIKQ ICQ CRQZM

By looking at the message so far it now becomes obvious that **Q = E** which will give the message: **I LIKE ICE CREZM.** It is not difficult to work out what **Z** stands for!

What would you get if you crossed a carrier pigeon with a woodpecker?

A bird that knocked before it delivered the message.

93

If you are trying to crack a code, try counting the frequency of a certain letter. the letter that occurs most in English is the letter **E,** or if a symbol or sign keeps appearing, there is a possibility that it stands for **E.** The letter that appears the second highest number of times is **T.** Once you have found those two letters you should find it easier to break the code.

Here are the rest of the letters in the alphabet in the order in which they are most used: **A, O, I, N, R, S, H, D, L, C, U, M, P, F, G, Y, B, W, K, V, J, Q, X, Z.**

If a fellow agent sneezes loudly three times it means, "**Get out quickly, you've been spotted.**"

When you decode messages, **accuracy** is more important than **speed.**

What four letters does a coder use when he spots decoder?

0-I-C-U.

94

Star Track

A visit to your local library to do some research on astronomy is time well spent. It will prevent you losing your way at night!

The stars are signs that appear on clear nights to show you the way.

Obtain from your library a book of flags from around the world. Then if you see a flag on a ship or on the side of a plane you will know immediately which country it comes from.

Polaris (the North Star) will always tell you which direction is north.

 People often used to send newspapers through the mail with pinpricks under letters and words so that a message could be read. Coders often put pinpricks under words in newspapers today when they wish to pass on a secret message.

You can fool a cipher clerk by reducing whole sentences to single code words. But if you also send the code word in a cipher, you really baffle them! How can they decode this message—19 1 21 19 1 7 5 19? Only you and your friends will know the code word is SAUSAGES in a number cipher.

If your mission involves some research into history do not be fooled into believing that something happened on **September 10, 1752,** because it didn't! Believe it or not, that day simply did not exist! This is because on September 2, 1752, the calendar was changed and jumped straight ahead to September 14. So you will now know that there are twelve days in history on which absolutely nothing happened!

There are many signs that can be scratched on the ground to give your contact a signal. They are based on signals usually drawn on the ground in large white letters to pilots in aircraft whose radio contact has broken down.

A letter **Y** means **yes, N** means **no, F** means **I need food,** and **LL** means **All is well.**

What's a twack?

Something a twain runs on.

What game do two coders like to play on a train journey?

I-spy.

What happened to the messenger who took a train home?

The master coder made him take it back.

A special sign for your code club to enter the room could be when you play a particular tune on the piano or put on a certain record. A member can remain hidden until he or she hears the music as a sign to enter.

If you are being watched, you are said to be **ILL.**

Any information that is so secret that only a few chosen people know it is called **CLASSI-FIED INFORMATION.**

An easy but very effective method of passing messages is to take an old newspaper and **write your message in the blank squares of a crossword puzzle.** Write your message in the squares going downwards, filling in the words across with other meaningless words. No one will bother to even look at a crossword that appears to have been completed.

 What do you call a frog spy?

A croak and dagger agent.

A general message to everyone in your code ring is called an APB, which means an "**All points bulletin.**"

 If you see a large "X" scratched on the ground, it is a sign meaning, "**Do not proceed.**"

Dial-a-Code
and More Home Modes

When you talk to your friends and family on the telephone always speak clearly and spell any words that might be misunderstood. To do this there is a special **international telephone and telegraph code** that is used all over the world. For example, if you had to spell out the word **SUSPECT** you would say:

SIERRA—UNCLE—SIERRA—PAPA— ECHO—CHARLIE—TANGO

Here is the international alphabet code:

A	ALPHA	N	NOVEMBER
B	BRAVO	O	OSCAR
C	CHARLIE	P	PAPA
D	DELTA	Q	QUEBEC
E	ECHO	R	ROMEO
F	FOXTROT	S	SIERRA
G	GOLF	T	TANGO
H	HOTEL	U	UNCLE
I	INDIA	V	VICTOR
J	JULIET	W	WHISKEY
K	KILO	X	X-RAY
L	LIMA	Y	YANKEE
M	MIKE	Z	ZULU

If you are going to telephone a message to a contact, let the telephone ring a couple of times, replace the receiver, and then dial again. This will give the contact a signal and he will know that it is you at the other end.

Your voice can be disguised over the telephone by holding your nose while you speak.

A code machine can be made using two discs of cardboard, one slightly smaller than the other. On the larger of the two, write the letters of the alphabet in a clockwise direction; on the smaller one write them in a counterclockwise direction. Put the two discs together, the smaller on top of the larger, and fasten them together through the center with a paper fastener.

To send a message simply choose a letter of the alphabet, **P** for example. Turn the letter **P** on the small wheel until it is against **A** on the big wheel. Spell out your message (keeping the wheel in this position) taking each letter in turn on the big wheel and writing down the corresponding letter on the small wheel. The wheel will give you 26 different codes, one for every letter of the alphabet. When you write the code, put the letter **P** first so that your contact knows how to decipher the message.

The **shopping list code** will never be cracked. It seems like an ordinary shopping list, but it is really a secret code.

A shopping list code could look like this:

> 7 **Bananas**
> 4 **Custards**
> 1 **Orange**
> 4 **Peppers**

This list looks innocent enough, but the numbers by the side tell you that if you count that number of letters in each word you will get a message. The seventh letter of bananas is S, the fourth of custard is T, the first letter of orange is O, and the fourth letter of peppers is P. Already we have the word **STOP** which is the beginning of a message. To practice this code make your own shopping list and finish what you think the message might be.

The **Box cipher** involves writing your message in a box. Draw a box with at least 25 squares and write your message with one letter in each square. You can write the message in a clockwise direction, counterclockwise, from left to right, and you could also write the message in any code you wish, too, so that it is difficult for anyone to decipher.

Take your message:
THERE IS NO BOMB NOW

It can look like this:

Clockwise	Counter-clockwise	Left to right
T H E R	B O N S	T H E R
M B N E	O W O I	E I S N
O W O I	M B N E	O B O M
B O N S	T H E R	B N O W

Decipher this secret message:

I O D U
A T I I
M I S S
N N G E

The message is read downwards.

It reads: I AM NOT IN DISGUISE

The foot cut from an old stocking is an excellent cap to wear under a wig to keep your own hair perfectly flat.

The **Inventory cipher** has been used for centuries. Simply make up an inventory, or list of items. In front of each item you place a number to tell your contact which letter of the word will give him or her the message.

An **Inventory cipher** looks like this:

INVENTORY	MESSAGE
5 Trunks	5 TrunKs
2 Tents	2 TEnts
4 Covers	4 CovErs
1 Pillow	1 Pillow
2 Basins	2 BAsins
1 Water Jug	1 Water Jug
2 Lamps	2 LAmps
4 Trays	4 TraYs

KEEP AWAY

Papers and maps can be hidden under mattresses and carpets.

The **Typewriter cipher** is very popular. If you have a typewriter then you can create your own cipher by substituting a symbol for each letter of the alphabet like this:

A .	H $	O ( )	V ;
B ..	I —	P *	W (-)
C ...	J &	Q ?	X "'
D !	K '	R +	Y ÷
E "	L ,	S =	Z ***
F /	M (	T %	
G @	N)	U :	

A message would then look like this:

.. " (-) . + "   ( ) /   & ( ) $)

Which reads: BEWARE OF JOHN

Decipher this secret message:

. ; ( ) — !   % $ "   * . + '   % ( ) ! . ÷

It reads: AVOID THE PARK TODAY

Why did the bald messenger throw away his keys?

Because he didn't have any locks.

106

Shady Shades

In Germany a black eye is called a "blue eye."

Which famous spy was red, tasty, and delicious in a salad?

Tomata Hari.

Cat's eyes appear to glow in the dark because they reflect the light.

Develop *your* own code with colored handkerchiefs. A red handkerchief in your top pocket could mean **danger**, green could mean **all is well**, etc.

A flesh colored balloon cut in half and stretched over your head can give you the appearance of being bald. The effect looks much better if you powder carefully around the edge to make it blend in with your skin.

In Florida, if you see flags flying with red and black squares in the center it means that there is going to be a hurricane.

Colored pencils in your pocket can be used to convey messages. Use different combinations of colors for each message. For example, a red, yellow and blue pencil in your top pocket will mean "**Follow me back to headquarters.**"

What is brown, hairy and wears dark glasses?

A coconut in disguise.

If you need a map of the area it can be embroidered as a pattern on a scarf. Or if you cannot sew, then an ordinary piece of white cloth can have the map drawn on it with brightly colored soft-tip pens and worn as a very colorful scarf.

The color used for danger in scientific laboratories is not red but **bright yellow.** Many fire departments are now painting their engines bright yellow.

 A red handkerchief hanging on a clothesline means "**DANGER.**"

 A green handkerchief on a clothesline means "**IT'S SAFE TO COME IN.**"

What is blue, runs on wheels, and eats grass?

A bus.
P.S. I lied about the grass.

 What is as big as an elephant, but doesn't weigh anything?

An elephant's shadow.

Whoever **always** wears dark glasses usually takes a dim view of things!

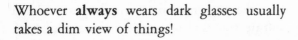

When you follow someone, you are known as the **shadow.** You can trail anyone for very long periods of time, frequently in disguise, so that you'll never be spotted.

 Squirrel is a Greek word meaning **"SHADOW TAIL."**

Always carry a large white handkerchief with you. Should an emergency arise you can always hide your face in it by pretending to blow your nose.

If walking along a muddy river bank, find two large leaves and walk on those, moving them into position each time you take a step. This way you will not leave any footprints.

You can give yourself a rosier complexion by rubbing rouge on your cheeks.

What happened to the spy who couldn't tell putty from oatmeal?

His windows fell out.

Infrared film can film invisible rays and things not normally visible to the naked eye. It has the added advantage of being able to film through mist. So if you are out on a foggy day you can still film a clear picture of the surroundings.

If you are going out trailing someone, wear a brightly colored sweater and carry another one of a different color in your bag. If you are spotted at any time you can quickly change sweaters and you will look completely different.

Another name for a shadow is a **tail**.

 Ultraviolet light, sometimes known as black light, can be used to detect enemy messages written in invisible ink.

A little tomato sauce on a bandage will make it look as if you have had a particularly nasty accident, and a secret document can be hidden underneath the bandage, because no one will dare look there!

The three-toed sloth disguises itself by allowing its body to be covered by a layer of tiny plants.

 A spy who specializes in photography is called a **Peep.**

The human eye can distinguish between two million different colors.

 Two thousand years ago in Ancient Egypt secret agents had messages tattooed on their heads. Unfortunately, to read the message their heads had to be shaved!

Bluff Stuff

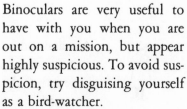

Binoculars are very useful to have with you when you are out on a mission, but appear highly suspicious. To avoid suspicion, try disguising yourself as a bird-watcher.

A secret code ring will help you with communications. All you need is a piece of wire, a bent paper clip, or even an old curtain ring—anything that can be made in a ring and slipped over your finger. Onto this ring, place three or four colored beads or tubes of cardboard that you have colored yourself. You must then develop your own code.

If, for example, you place the red bead at the top (the other three will be on the other side of the ring and under your finger, so not seen) it will mean "**Danger,**" a blue bead could mean "**You are being followed,**" etc. You can also use combinations of beads so that red and blue together means something totally different. In this way you will get hundreds of combinations. You can even make the code more comprehensive by wearing it on different fingers: for example, on your *little* finger it could be all the *danger* messages; on your *second* finger it could be *code* names, and so on. You can do exactly the same thing with a code bracelet or necklace. But do not have more than six beads. Otherwise the codes will be too complicated and your contact could easily get the message wrong.

 Alexander the Great had several very large helmets made which were left lying around. He hoped that the enemy would think his army was made up of giants.

A daily newspaper can be used to successfully send messages to a contact. Take a pin and prick under a number on the date, under an 8, for example. When the contact picks up the paper and sees the dot under the 8 he will realize that the message is on page 8. On that page you will have pricked holes under certain words to spell out your message. To read your message the contact can hold the page up to the light. He will see quite clearly which words have a pinprick under them.

Disguise your walk by taking very big strides and swinging your arms as you go.

A useful bulletin board can be made for your headquarters out of polystyrene. A section can be attached to the wall. You can pin notices, messages, and maps to communicate with your members.

A sling on your arm can provide a very useful hiding place for a small tape recorder.

 A hat can make a great hiding place and will also provide a disguise.

An umbrella can be used to hide secret messages. Open the umbrella and attach the rolled paper around the shaft with an elastic band. Close the umbrella again. The papar is safely concealed.

A secret hiding place for small objects is a very large old book that *nobody* wants any more. Cut a large square hole in the center of every page in the book. This will make the book hollow, although from the outside it will look like an ordinary book. Your most secret objects can be hidden inside the book and the book can be kept on your bookshelves.

Search your headquarters carefully for loose floorboards. Underneath you might find a cavity. If it is small, you can hide valuable documents and equipment underneath. Then cover the floorboard with a rug.

A stamp can be made by cutting a potato in half and carefully cutting out a design, perhaps a skull and crossbones, or a small symbol of your own, even your own initials. When you have cut it, press it onto an ink pad and print it on any paper you wish. This will give all your papers a special *identification mark* which will be impossible for anyone to forge.

If you take a drawer out of a chest or sideboard, you can often find a small cavity at the back. This space could prove to be a good hiding place for small objects.

A useful piece of equipment is your own thumb. Measure the distance from the first joint to the tip in inches and remember it. You can then use it as a measure.

A false pocket to your jacket can be a useful hiding place for small messages. Take a square of fabric slightly smaller than the inside of your pocket. Hold it inside your pocket and sew around the three sides (leaving the top open). You can now put objects in the compartment nearest to you and close the top with a safety pin. You will now be able to use your ordinary pocket as usual. And no one, even if they put their hand inside, will notice the false pocket!

Hide documents or identity cards in an ordinary book. Simply glue two edges of two pages together to form a pocket, leaving the top open. Papers can then be slipped into this pocket and the book can be put on your bookshelves.

If a messenger puts his finger in his left ear it means **"Keep away."**

If he puts his finger in his right ear it means **"All is well."**

What do secret agents in a nuclear installation eat?

Nuclear fission chips.

A hollow candle is a clever piece of equipment. Take an ordinary white wax candle; cut off about 1¼ inches from the top and 1¼ inches from the bottom. Make a tube of white cardboard to look like a candle. Push the pieces of real candle into the top and bottom so that it looks like a complete candle. Only you will know of the secret compartment.

Anything you hide behind—whether a building, tree, or fence—is called a **COVER**.

A reliable compass using a magnetized needle can be made by placing a leaf or piece of tissue paper on water so that it floats. Carefully lay the needle onto the leaf. Now, very carefully, push the leaf under the water. The needle should remain afloat and will swing round to point north. Practice in a dish of water at your headquarters or home.

If you are following bicycle tracks and come across two and do not know which to follow, the most recent will be the one that has cut over the top of the other.

Keep any empty tissue boxes. They provide good storage space for equipment.

 Always keep a copy of your code book hidden in a very secret place. If you lost or accidentally destroyed the original, you would still have a copy.

A piece of garden cane (used to support flowers and plants) can be a useful place for hiding secret messages. Take a screwdriver to widen the hole in the center. Then roll your message up very tightly and slip it into the cane.

 When imprisoned, **Mary Queen of Scots** received secret messages that were sent to her in barrels of ale.

A highly successful **compass** can be made using a sewing needle. Be careful not to prick yourself. All you have to do is rub the needle a few times against a magnet, always from the *point* to the *eye* of the needle. This rubbing will magnetize it. When you get lost simply hang the needle onto a piece of thread. When it stops spinning, the direction in which the *eye* is pointing will be north.

A useful piece of equipment to have is a *small piece of chalk*. With it, secret symbols and codes can be left on walls, lampposts, gravestones, etc. When your contact has received the message, he can easily rub it out.

Watch television plays and see how well-known actors have changed their voice, mannerisms, and appearance. It might give you a few tips when you are disguising yourself.

An effective burglar alarm can be made out of some old tin cans. Punch holes in the bottom of three or four cans. Thread some string through them and hang them behind your door. If someone opens the door stealthily and hopes to creep in unnoticed, he will find it impossible. As soon as the door is opened, it will knock the cans and sound the alarm.

To give yourself a *black eye,* brush some blue and grey eyeshadow around your eye and smooth it gently with your finger to make it look like a bruise.

Animals have a very acute sense of smell. So if you are trailing an animal, or if your rival has a dog, be certain to remain *downwind.* If you do not, the wind will blow your scent towards him and your quarry will know that he is being followed.

Where can you find the secret page numbers?

(To find codes and ciphers, see Contents, page 5)

Index